To Michelle Dunwoody,
Cultivate joy in all you
do. It will sustain you.
Peace and blessings.

CULTIVATING

Joy

Sheltering Within During Life's Storms

Rosell L. Jenkins, PhD

ISBN's

Perfect Binding — 978-0-9995144-0-5
eBook/.MOBI — 978-0-9995144-2-9
eBook/.ePub — 978-0-9995144-1-2

www.mwsolutionspc.com

Editor — Faye Walker
Cover Design — Ken Fraser

Printed in The United States of America

Dedication

To joyful souls everywhere, who are ever
reflecting and embracing the light.

This book is dedicated to my son,
Christopher,
for teaching me so much about love and
inspiring me to intentionally cultivate joy
on a daily basis.

Table of Contents

Acknowledgements   9
Introduction   12
Chapter 1   Joy Even as the Storm Intensifies   21
Chapter 2   Finding Your Joy   29
Chapter 3   Maintaining Joy in the Face of
            Devastation or Loss   37
Chapter 4   Allowing Others to Impact Your Joy . .   51
Chapter 5   Expect Joy and Wonder Each Day . . .   63
Chapter 6   Smell the Flowers, Don't Linger in
            the Poop   73
Chapter 7   Believe in Your Ability to Know
            What Works Best For You   83
Chapter 8   Remove Obstacles to Your Joy   91
Chapter 9   Courageously, Boldly, Freely Give
            and Receive Love   105
Chapter 10 A Joy Tune-Up — Help!
            I've Lost My Joy   119
Chapter 11 Conclusion   131
            About the Author   139
            References   143

Acknowledgements

The idea for this book originated from my personal storms. To get through those, I learned to intentionally cultivate joy. Now, I am grateful for those difficult times, situations, and people that were vital to my growth in this area and for serving as an inspiration for this book. I am most thankful to Spirit for guiding and sustaining me through all things.

I want to acknowledge my SCORE mentor, David Lurie, encouraged me to get this book off of my computer and get it published.

I have wonderful friends, and they make it easy for me to smile and laugh, even during my storms. Many of them also inspired me or anchored me over the years. They include my Kindred group in Houston (Gia, Olivia, Tiffany, Tammy, and Milli), Glennis Foster, Rosalyn Comer, Ted Brown, Heather Hurd,

Nikki Coleman, Marlene Dawkins, Kamau, and AD. I could not have or ask for a better tribe.

I am also thankful to my aunt, Regina Curry, for nurturing my love of reading and words at a very early age. I am thankful to my aunts Loretta and Devarieste Curry for always encouraging and supporting me in all my endeavors.

My mother, Evelyn Elliott, has always encouraged me and believed in me. I am especially grateful to her for her unconditional love and support. My grandmother, Elmira Curry, set a great example of "being content wherever you are." She has taught me much about inner joy. My grandfather, Elcue Curry, is deceased but he always encouraged me (and I believe still does) to do and give my best. My deceased aunt, Vanessa Curry, was one of the most radiant beings that I have ever known, and I appreciate her glowing smile and her spirit.

Dr. Nicole Coleman, Glennis Foster, and Dr. Terrlyn L. Curry Avery offered guidance and read portions of my manuscript and I am especially thankful for their willingness to do so.

One of my dearest friends, Gretchen Generett, serves as such a great model for me of generosity

Rosell L. Jenkins, PhD

of spirit. She has supported me in numerous ways and I could not have brought this book to life without her belief in me and support.

Still, this book probably would not have come to life without the nudging, nagging, and love of Dr. Terrlyn L. Curry Avery and Jerome Murphy. They would tag team to light a fire under me. Terrlyn was also very helpful in guiding me through the writing and publishing process. Jerome has been one of my biggest emotional supporters and my most ardent cheerleader. They both motivated me every step of the way. My gratitude knows no bounds.

Finally, I am thankful to my son, Christopher, for his patience with me during this project that took time away from him. I'm also thankful to all that helped care for him while I worked on this book, especially his grandmother Elease Jenkins, and my neighbor, Ansa Williams.

It took a village to bring this book to life and you all have been mine! I am so very grateful!!!

———————

Introduction

Despite the leanness of my bank account and cash on hand, I am in good spirits as I run out early on a Saturday morning, with my son in tow, to complete an errand. It's a sunny day and I'm feeling healthy and happy, and so is my son. I am reveling in these good feelings and feeling grateful as I turn down an aisle with a row of cars to find a parking space. I pass up a few because they look too tight. I find one and slowly ease in the pick-up I am driving.

Then... I stop. What is that sound and what is that feeling? It feels like I hit something. I move a bit more and there's that sound again, like metal scraping into metal. I realize with a sinking feeling I have hit the car in the space next to me even though I was so sure I was turning wide enough to clear it, and even though I passed up spaces to find one that I could get in with no problem.

　　　　　　　　Rosell L. Jenkins, PhD

I get out of my vehicle and see I have indeed hit another vehicle. I notice the vehicle I have hit is a luxury SUV. I immediately begin to apologize profusely to the man who was already out of the vehicle. He was paying little attention to me as he was in the process of calling someone. I hear him telling the person that someone just hit her car. After a few minutes have passed, in which I continue to apologize, a person exits from one of the stores and makes her way to where we are in the parking lot. It is apparent from the scowl on her face that she is very upset. She lets out a string of profanities and insults directed towards me and my driving. I apologize again, in an effort to calm her, and I let her know I will do whatever is necessary to repair her vehicle. I also draw her attention to my child, my two-and-a-half-year-old son, who is still strapped into his car seat, taking in the situation.

She was difficult to calm, despite my remaining calm and composed and attempting to disarm her by fully cooperating. I gave her my insurance information. I gave her my business card and phone number. I even waited while she called the police and had them arrive, despite them saying prior to their arrival that there was nothing they could do that we had not done. Both vehicles remained in driving condition, and we were in a private parking lot.

Although I maintained my composure while I was at the scene, I had worked myself into an anxious frenzy by the time I arrived home. In that time I had gone over and over again in my head, what would ensue. I was temporarily driving my ex-husband's vehicle as I searched for an affordable used car to purchase. I had been driving it for a couple of months now and had been extremely careful while driving it. I could only imagine what he would say. I thought about how expensive it would be for me to obtain insurance for the yet-to-be-purchased vehicle. I even thought about how his insurance rates would increase. I had built up an avalanche of potential negative outcomes.

Frankly, I was in quite a funk. A friend later came to visit, and I was still in a funk. I hadn't yet told my ex-husband, and I didn't want to tell him. I had been berated by the woman whom I had hit, and I was not up to hearing what I believed would be the grief he would give me about the accident. My friend attempted

Rosell L. Jenkins, PhD

to get my mind off the incident, but I remained consumed with thoughts about the accident and all of the terrible things that would now happen as a result. Finally, she reminded me of my general optimistic outlook and approach to life. She said, "Rosell, you can't be Miss Joy and Light and let one little accident throw you off course," or something similar to that. It was her exasperation with me as well as what she said that finally drew a smile from me.

She reminded me I have been able to maintain my joy in the face of much worse things. In fact, the idea for this book came about when I was going through a crisis in my marriage. Some of my other "much worse" things included my eventual divorce and my aunt's long battle with the cancer that ultimately took her life. I had intentionally cultivated and maintained inner joy even in the face of these storms.

So can you! I'm going to share with you how I was able to do that. I know we all have different crises that can take us to some dark places. If we aren't able to cultivate joy for ourselves, we can get stuck in those places. Everyone deserves joy and light in their lives. I don't have a monopoly on it, but I do have some expertise in cultivating it. My work as a clinical psychologist and coach helping other people to connect to experiences that bring them joy and to develop or deepen their inner joy, in addition to my personal experiences, have given me insights on joy. In the chapters that follow, I will share some of my professional and personal experiences to provide tips for cultivating your joy every single day—no matter the severity of your storm.

———◆◆◆———

CULTIVATING

Joy

Sheltering Within During Life's Storms

1
CHAPTER

Life isn't about waiting for the storm to pass...It's about learning to dance in the rain.

—Vivian Greene

Joy Even as the Storm Intensifies

Marriage *is challenging*. Trite, clichéd, true words that are often spoken and heard. Thus, I was not particularly surprised when my marriage encountered inclement weather. Despite this, I was surprised when my husband told me one day he had filed for divorce. What I remember of that moment is I didn't immediately respond, because I just felt gripped with this overwhelming fear. Some of my thoughts may have been:

> *What now?*
> *Am I going to be alone?*

What did I do or not do?
How will I live?
What will people think?
What will I say?
What about our daughter?

My thoughts were racing and my heart was pounding. I decided to leave and go to a nearby park. At first, I just sat there. Then, I began to write all I was thinking and feeling. After putting pen to paper to write my husband wanted a divorce, I wrote:

> *I'm at the lake…It's nice. The trees, the water, the ducks, even the noise of the crickets. Their hums rise in full crescendo and then it lowers to a soft murmur. The kids playing and screeching in amusement. Sounds of joy. Sounds of life. Sounds of life… Being here connects me to Spirit, to nature, to all things. I feel love. I am love. I'll be ok.*

After that, I just asked for peace, protection, and acceptance of whatever was to come. That calmed me and I was able to return home and to return to myself—courageous, loving, assured, and faith-filled.

Rosell L. Jenkins, PhD

Over the next few months as my husband and I tried to weather the storm and determine if we would do this together or apart, I would return to this day in the park and the solace I was able to find in those moments. This was certainly a difficult time in which to cultivate or maintain joy, but I made it my mission to do so. I knew that whatever happened between me and my husband, I was going to need joy—a sense of inner contentment and stability—to get me through it all.

Early in my marriage, I used to tell my husband when I thought he was intentionally irritating me that I was not going to let him steal my joy. Thus, writing when I was facing such a serious crisis in my marriage was my reminder to myself of what was my right, even in the face of a faltering marriage. The idea for this book was borne out of this difficult time in my life. When I began writing this book, many years ago, we weathered that marital storm and remained married.

A lot has happened since that time. Anyone who is reading this book knows life can sometimes seem like continuous preparation for varying storms with different degrees of severity. My husband and

I ultimately divorced. At the time we separated, we had a child who was a bit shy of six months old. Navigating life as a single mother of an infant, while running a business and learning to live on one income as opposed to two, required me to work even harder at cultivating joy.

Some people think of living a life of peace, filled with contentment and joy as boring. Many people are unaccustomed to feeling joy. They are going through life, accomplishing tasks, serving others, and not really taking time to think about whether they are enjoying their life. When I am coaching, or providing therapy to people, a common refrain I hear is "I just want to be happy." Yet when I ask what this means or what happiness would look like for them, they are often unable to answer this question, to even come up with a single thing that is a component of their happiness. I am aware, in these moments, that "happiness," as referred to by most people, is tied to a thing or activity that elicits positive feelings. I find it surprising and sad that people are unable to identify even one thing that elicits happiness in them. Social science and more recent theories indicate that a more constant sense of happiness is derived from meaning and satisfaction in one's life. Perhaps, people's inability to identify a single source of happiness stems from some deeper knowledge that a temporary "hit" of pleasure or happiness does not change how they feel overall.

A more permanent state of happiness is akin to inner joy does not come from someone else or some thing. This is an internal feeling that comes from a sense of self-satisfaction, wherever you are and if you are with someone or alone. Does that mean you are never going to feel down? No. It means that you know when you feel down you will come back up again and you won't think or feel like you are drowning and that drowning might not be such a bad idea. You know you have a lifeline and you know how to avail yourself of it.

What I want you to know, and the lessons I have learned from my experiences as well as listening to and observing others, is that cultivating the practice of joy made going through my divorce and the ensuing intensified life/work juggles, co-parenting differences, and financial challenges less challenging. Through it all, I was able to stay steady, assured, and loving. *I know for sure that joy is maintained through practice.* Your circumstances don't matter. Anyone, **EVEN YOU**, can have a joyful life. As many people are unaware of how to even begin accessing a more sustained, inner joy, the next several chapters will provide steps for accessing your joy.

———•••••———

Rosell L. Jenkins, PhD

2

CHAPTER

The most wasted of all days is one without laughter.

—e.e. cummings

Finding Your Joy

Seeing my son's genuine, ear-to-ear smile
Watching dogs frolic and play
Feeling the sun on my face
Leisurely savoring a good book
Taking a hot, scented bath
Hiking a trail that ends in a spectacular waterfall
Taking a bite of dark chocolate with caramel and nuts

All these are pleasurable experiences for me. Pleasure is considered by many social scientists to be a component of happiness. Pleasure is associated with positive emotions, which is what people commonly think of when they say they feel "happy." However, pleasure or the positive emotions associated with being "happy" can be fleeting. Even when I am not engaged in a pleasurable activity, a sense of deep contentment, ease, and feeling of security remains with me. This is derived from my cultivation of joy. What comes to mind when you think of joy? Do you have joy in your life?

Joy is described by many as an internal state of serenity/contentment, sustainable even in the midst of changing circumstances. Even though joy is not dependent on outer circumstances, joy is not automatic or permanent. For many, getting to an internal state of joy may begin with bringing into awareness those experiences which they enjoy and the aspects of self that are appreciated and valued. This may differ for people based on their interests, temperaments, and personalities. In my enjoyable moments, I am happy, fully present and my senses are engaged in whatever I am doing. For example, when I take a bubble bath, I usually have music playing and I am focused on the feel of hot water on my skin, the sound of the music, the scent of fragrance or oil used in my bath. I am thinking

Rosell L. Jenkins, PhD

of nothing else in that moment but how wonderfully relaxing the experience is. I am always grateful and elated in that moment. Having a young child and a busy life, I know finding time to linger in a bath feels indulgent, and I thoroughly enjoy the experience and feel appreciative to have it. While I enjoy that moment, I am able to recognize that the temporary joy or pleasure that comes from this experience is distinct from my inner joy. My inner joy, the sense of serenity that comes from knowing all is well in every moment, is retained long after the experience has passed. I am able to maintain my inner joy because I can appreciate and value whatever experience I am having. Even when my experiences are unpleasant, I know there is some value in the experience, even when that value eludes me in the exact moment of the experience. Gratitude helps me cultivate and maintain my joy.

What is universal about inner joy, I believe, is that its foundation is based on a belief that life and people are good and good is intended for all to be extended and shared by all. If we think our lives should be joyful and are able to recognize those things that bring us joy, we are more likely to experience and notice joy in our lives. We also are more likely to know the value of cultivating joy.

Spend a moment right now thinking about one thing you really value. This thing could be your mate, your child, your car, your position, etc. Now, think about what you do to care for that which you value. For example, if you value a person, you probably engage in loving and protective acts. If it is an item, you may insure it. If it is your position or title, you give your best work to maintain it. Think about why you do these things and the value your actions suggest. If you do not give the same time and attention to your joy, perhaps you don't value it in the same way. Maybe, you think you will experience joy spontaneously and maintain that joy without any effort, without caring for it and attending to it. You may not even be certain you are worthy of joy. If any of these thoughts come to mind, know that they are misperceptions. You **ABSOLUTELY** deserve joy and your joy is so precious that it requires care, nurturing, and protection!

First, you have to know what fills you with a sense of you and contentment. If you are unaware of what brings you joy, ask yourself the following questions:

Rosell L. Jenkins, PhD

- When am I most open to possibility?
- What excites and energizes me?
- When did I last feel genuine enthusiasm?
- When am I most creative? How do I express that creativity? If you do not express it, what would be the ideal way for you to express your creativity?
- Do you share creativity, energy, or enthusiasm with others?

Reflect on these questions and your answers. If you had trouble identifying your joy, perhaps you need to spend time around someone you consider joyful. You may even need to spend some time reflecting on when you last felt joyful. You may have to go back as far as childhood to reach this awareness. If you do not believe you have ever experienced joyful moments, it may be that you discounted these moments or did not recognize this state. Perhaps, you have never experienced even a fleeting state of joy. If that is the case, continue on this journey with me. Together, we will discover, activate, or connect you to your joy.

Along the way, if you find you have been squelching your joy or experiencing it in isolation, you will begin to share it with others. A state of joy is illuminating and inviting. You will feel drawn to those people that are joyful and your expression of joy will draw others to you.

———•••••———

Rosell L. Jenkins, PhD

3
CHAPTER

The deeper that sorrow carves into your being, the more joy you can contain.

—Kahlil Gibran

Maintaining Joy in the Face of Devastation or Loss

As I mentioned in the introduction to the book, when I first began writing about joy and intentionally practicing the cultivation of it, I was writing as a way to help me process and understand my feelings around my husband seeking a divorce. During this time, a beloved aunt was also battling a cancer from which she ultimately died. Spending time with my aunt during her illness left me with many thoughts and questions but very little joy. For instance, I questioned why she had to suffer. As I was experiencing the layered heaviness of the turmoil in my marriage and the anguish of my aunt's illness, it seemed that any additional bad news was too much to bear. I found it hard to watch the news, because news stories about tragedies, particularly people mistreating others, heightened my feelings of sadness and helplessness.

In the midst of editing this book on joy, the worst mass shooting in the history of America occurred. Writing about this, as did listening to the news coverage, returned me to a dark, sad place. This tragedy stopped me in my tracks. I am certain the shock and paralysis I felt was magnified significantly for those personally impacted by the loss. For many people like me, sitting home, hearing, or reading about the murder of innocent people, who presumably simply expected to enjoy a night of dancing and entertainment at a nightclub, was also devastating. From my professional experience as a psychologist, I know that when tragedies like the Orlando shooting occur, people often feel unsafe. Moreover, tragedies of any magnitude can erode one's faith in humanity, and lead to agonizing, unanswerable questions, among other things.

After this tragedy occurred, I had trouble connecting to my joy. Finding the motivation to think

　　　　　　　Rosell L. Jenkins, PhD

or write about joy was even more challenging. Thinking about the loss of life, the senseless violence, and the state of humanity, I felt disheartened, discouraged, and angry. I asked myself if writing about joy was even worthwhile. I thought if things like this continue to happen so frequently, is the world really changing, as I like to believe? Are we truly able to have joy, peace, and contentment in this life? Even though I know that statistics and researchers, such as Harvard psychologist Stephen Pinker, indicate that our world really is more peaceful today, it seems hard to believe when we are inundated with media stories highlighting one horrendous event after another. When we are deluged daily with negativity when we access the media, our problems can seem so vast.

When tragedy occurs, on a small or large scale, people feel many emotions. Sadness, anger, and despair are natural responses. These emotions are components of the healing process, and one does not have to feel pressure to not feel them or return to a joyful state immediately. That is unreasonable and unhealthy. It is important to own and acknowledge your feelings. When loss occurs, even a loss of beliefs, taking time to examine your feelings and grieve that loss is important. It can be useful to talk to other people. You may find it useful to speak with a spiritual advisor, a trusted friend, psychologist, or other mental health counselor.

When faced with trials or storms in your life, it is important to remember that cultivating and maintaining joy does not mean you will not encounter or have challenges in your life. What it means is that experiencing a challenge or a tragedy will not permanently rob you of your joy. Often, you will still be able to experience moments of joy even in the midst of a challenge. Of course, that is entirely dependent on the magnitude of the challenge.

In my professional life and when accessing the media, I hear countless stories of people's pain and sad circumstances. A question I am frequently asked is how I am able to hear about people's pain on a daily basis and not be in a constant state of depression. The short answer is I know in order to do the work I do that I have to make attending to my feelings and retaining my inner joy a priority. One of the ways I do that is limit my access to social media and other media. I intentionally "dose" myself with humor by

Rosell L. Jenkins, PhD

watching comedies. When friends try to tell me about the latest television serials they find spellbinding and they contain violence or are too "heavy," I let them know that is not for me.

Also, doing the work I do as a coach and a psychologist also encourages and energizes me. Despite the painful experiences my clients share, I hear about how people love and overcome, and I see how hard they work to be and give the best of themselves. For example, I have seen people who have experienced physical abuse and neglect that I could not have imagined consciously look for models of love and caring. They do this to find healthier examples of parenting than they observed in their homes. Hearing the stories of my clients fuels my dedication and determination. I know joy is intended for all of us and it makes me sad for those who do not have it. Not having joy in my life does not honor those who do not have it. Staying in a place of sadness, anger, impatience, or disgust does not help me or those who have experienced violence, misery, or tragedy in their lives.

It is also tempting to think the problems that we hear about and see, particularly in the media, are too large for us to tackle and to feel overwhelmed by their magnitude. I sometimes feel that way when I hear about stories of random violence, political chaos, mistreatment/degradation of people for any reason, and many other issues. However, I know part of my cultivating and maintaining joy comes from taking action to ensure I am doing my part to generate peace and harmony in my community and beyond.

Whenever I am faced with an issue/event that produces such strong negative feelings, I can choose to learn more about it, even though that may be very difficult emotionally. I can then determine what I can do to help bring about change in that situation. My effort may be small; but if I make an effort and others do as well, our combined efforts increase our effect and are powerful. A friend and colleague is a great example of this. She, like many others, myself included, felt devastated and disheartened by the shootings of unarmed black men by some police officers. She indicated that she felt helpless and powerless. She cried, shared her feelings with others, and then she acted. She contacted a group of women and asked them to send handwritten words

Rosell L. Jenkins, PhD

of comfort/love to the mothers, wives, partners of those men who had been killed. She wanted to offer love and community to these women. I was moved by her request and her thoughtfulness. We can always choose to act and to move beyond a place of powerlessness and hopelessness. Even when we meet significant challenges, responding to these challenges with hopefulness and perseverance, which helps to breed joy, is our choice.

Every day **you get to choose**. Many people think they do not have a choice or they feel stuck in their current life path. You are only limited by your imagination. Your lack of imagination combined with a lack of confidence produces a state of morass and this idea that you are stuck. While you may have a fleeting awareness of two or three probable solutions or outcomes to your current predicament, you get focused on THE SOLUTION. You believe this SOLUTION is the only thing that will bring you joy or peace. This SOLUTION usually takes the form of *if only I had another job* or *if only I had a (different) mate* or *if only I made more money* or *if only I lived in another place then everything would be perfect*. While all of those things are wonderful and great, what will bring you peace and joy is changing the way you view your problem and its solution.

In my years of seeing people in psychotherapy, I have seen people with wonderful mates, wonderful jobs, wonderful homes, and no financial concerns, yet they remain discontented, disgruntled, and dispirited. They have little or no joy in their life. Peace and contentment continues to elude them, despite their best efforts. Sometimes, they recall having felt joyful or happy but now feel disconnected from that joy. One of the comments I frequently hear from clients is "I feel like I have lost myself." What these people are communicating is they are out of touch with that which makes them feel most at peace and secure with themselves and their life—those things that bring joy.

The problem is often that a person is too focused on something that occurred in the past. This past negative event is believed to be impeding any present chance at lasting happiness or joy. They posit that only if this experience never happened, then they could attain joy. My work with many individuals presenting with this problem suggests this is untrue, as these people seem to be chasing temporary pleasure/

happiness. If temporary pleasure is the only component of their happiness, then they soon find another reason to be unhappy. Some other event or person is blamed for robbing them of their happiness/joy. Conversely, if it is not a past experience, then it is something in the present they are not getting that would bring them **true joy**. They may blame their lack of joy on a co-worker, a mate, a child, or a friend. Their joy is always someone else's responsibility. "If only I had some friends, then I would not be stuck at home alone all the time," one might say. The story that follows is a great example of how one of my former clients took action to intentionally cultivate joy in her life by changing her mood, outlook, and actions.

Sally had been widowed for a few years and her husband had been quite ill prior to his death. She was her husband's caretaker for the last years of his life, and it required all of her time, energy, and resources, by her accounts. When she initially came to see me, she was depressed, lonely, and not engaging much with life or anyone. She felt that so much of her time had been given to caretaking when her husband's health deteriorated and that she had lost herself in her marriage, even prior to her husband's illness. Sally indicated she no longer had a sense of what she enjoyed or what brought her pleasure. A component of her treatment involved helping her identify and begin engaging with people, places, or things she liked. I encouraged her to find a hobby, a group, or activity which she enjoyed. As she was very compliant with treatment recommendations, she began to engage more with a group for seniors and to reconnect with her friends.

Soon, an elderly gentleman expressed a romantic interest in Sally. She expressed trepidation about dating. She worried she was too old to date. She wondered what people she knew might think about her dating, if she began spending time with this gentleman. She worried that the gentleman was older than her. "What if some chronic illness befalls him and I have to care for him?" she asked. She also worried that her adult children might not be comfortable with the idea of her dating. Sally wondered if the man might want to get married, declaring that she was not interested in marrying again. In one of our sessions, she revealed that she had not even had intimate relations for many years with her husband prior to his death because of

Rosell L. Jenkins, PhD

his illness. Sally's worries (and hopes, I gently teased) about this prospect were numerous.

Sally, like many people, was allowing her past experiences to limit her belief about what was possible for her in the present. She also created a long list of potential future hazards for which she had no real basis, except her past fears. I am not sure what decision Sally would have made had we not been working together to challenge her fears and without my encouragement to act based on the information that she had at hand. I reminded her to remain in the present and to just slowly begin spending time with this man, to ascertain if that was enjoyable for her. Over time, she discovered that she quite enjoyed spending time with this gentleman and that they were very compatible. She even learned that he was in great physical health.

This relationship continued to progress over the time that I saw Sally. She blossomed, released her fears, and delighted in her present life with her companion. In fact, she eventually decided that she wanted to make a commitment to this gentleman. I saw them both on our last visit together and their genuine affection for each other was obvious. Sally was inspiring to me then and continues to be. Although she could have allowed her fears and past experiences to limit or stop her, she did not allow this. She made the effort to keep moving through her sadness, her loneliness, and her worries to create a life that was to her liking. She did not let her age or the ideas of others stop her from reclaiming her joy.

Sally's story is just one example of how changing your ideas about yourself and your life have the power to change whatever you are experiencing in your life. *The solution lies within you.* It is not about what is happening in your life that is the problem. It is what you are thinking about what is happening in your life. As Norman Vincent Peale wrote, "Change your thoughts and change your world."

———•••——

4

CHAPTER

When there is no enemy within, the enemies outside cannot hurt you.

—**African Proverb**

Allowing Others to Impact Your Joy

There are times when our joy is constrained by our interactions with others or our circumstances. Ask yourself these questions:

- *Do you only feel happy or worthwhile when you are receiving positive feedback from others?*
- *Do you feel unwanted and unlovable if you are not in a relationship?*
- *Do you worry that you have done something wrong if someone you admire or for whom you care snaps at you for no apparent reason?*

Do you have a "bad day" as a result of this interaction?

If you answered yes to any of the above questions, then you allow others to impact your joy. When you are intentionally cultivating and maintaining your joy, an important skill to learn is how to create a zone of protection for your joy. This zone of protection cannot be invaded or impacted by others' barbs, negativity, or rudeness. As you are going about your day-to-day activities and even relying on others to meet obligations during your day, you may encounter snags or obstacles that seem designed to take you out of your zone of joy. Having your protection activated will help prevent this. Your protection consists of your behavior and thoughts, which will be detailed much more in later chapters.

Staying in your zone of joy can be a challenge. I am aware of this, as I encounter many things that seem designed to move me out of this zone. Some of what I encounter has to do with my personality style and expectations. For example, I am aware I can be a bit of a taskmaster. If I encounter someone who is more laissez-faire regarding tasks and we have to work together, one of us is likely to be moved outside of our zone of joy, especially if we desire the other person to conform to our style or expectations.

For me to remain in my zone of joy, I may need to reconsider the importance I place on accomplishing tasks. That is to say, I may even need to alter my expectations of others. While I am aware I cannot change others, I know I can make an adjustment in my thoughts and attitudes. I know many people see this as "letting a person off the hook" or "making excuses for another's behavior." While that viewpoint can be taken, it is probably going to lead to you feeling more disgruntled and discontented, particularly if the problem is simply a matter of two people taking a different approach to accomplishing a task.

There will also be times when you will be taken outside of your joy zone because mutually-agreed to and reasonable obligations/expectations were not met. There will be times when people make promises and drop the ball. At these times, you will feel disappointed and frustrated. These are expected feelings. You may even feel angry. Again, protecting your zone of joy doesn't mean you won't feel any other emotion. That is unrealistic. When reasonable and mutually-agreed upon expectations are not met, to return to your zone of joy do the following:

- Express your disappointment, frustration or anger—appropriately and constructively.
- Discuss the incident that led to your feelings and discuss only that incident.
- Keep it concise.
- Say how you would like for the situation to be handled in the future.
- Then drop it. No nagging or holding grudges about the misdeed.

Following the above steps does not guarantee the other's behavior will change. It may not. You are expressing yourself so you can move beyond the incident and intentionally return to your place of joy despite experiencing a moment of frustration, resentment, anger, disappointment, etc. Remember, you always have control over how you feel and you get to decide if you want to stay in a place of negativity or move to a different state.

Many years ago, I was working with a client who was recounting how her spouse responded angrily to what she perceived as a neutral, non-offensive comment. She went on to say how her spouse's behavior and attitude changed and he stopped speaking to her. As she was talking about this, she became more incensed, remarking, "I decided that I was not approaching him, as I normally do. It's his problem. I am not making the effort. I get tired of making the first move and being the bigger person."

I have heard a variation of this comment numerous times. I have even thought it myself in the past. As I grew in consciousness and begin to actively commit to and practice the techniques that I shared with others, I focused more on what I needed to have peace in my life and less on what I thought others needed to do for me to feel or think a certain way. In the past, I have thought, "He/she made me feel like…" When I began focusing on maintaining peace in my life and cultivating joy, I changed this thought to "I choose to feel… Is this useful for me right now?"

In a perfect world in which we all had the same sunny personalities and dispositions and were all highly considerate of one another and loved ourselves supremely, we would rarely have conflict with others. If we did, whatever misunderstanding that was the source of this negative encounter would be resolved very quickly with easy, straightforward dialogue. Unfortunately, most of us do not reside in a home, work in a place, or live in a neighborhood with highly evolved, similarly-minded residents. We encounter people with varying moods, temperaments, and dispositions who encounter us with whatever is their current issue of the day. This person may be your boss, your spouse, a friend, or the person serving you coffee in the morning.

Let's say every encounter you have with this person evokes negative thoughts and emotions for you. For instance, every morning you greet this person cheerily and your cheery greeting is met with silence, a grunt, or "Why are you smiling and so happy?" Generally, this is said in an unmistakably snarky tone. Do you 1) tuck away your cheeriness and slouch away? Do you 2) snap, "I was in a good mood until I

Rosell L. Jenkins, PhD

spoke to you?" Or do you 3) continue smiling, feeling cheerful and move along with your day? If you do some variation of 1 or 2 each day and this has continued for some time, it may be time to make a behavioral change. If your thoughts and feelings as they relate to another person are frequently, sad, frustrated, stressed, or worried, you need to ask yourself some questions.

- Has feeling this way altered the situation?
- Has feeling this way altered me?
- Am I helping myself or this person by feeling this way?

If the answer to the latter is "No," then you want to make some changes in your life. Think about what you really need to be happy and at peace. Maybe, what you need is distance from a particular person, place, or thing. Your distance might come in the form of mental or emotional distance. Or it might actually take the form of physical distance.

You may be wondering what is mental or emotional distance. In the above scenario where a person is responding to a pleasant, cheery greeting with gruffness or rudeness, mental distance would simply mean not taking this response personally. If nothing has transpired between you and another person to evoke their negative response to you, to obtain mental distance and remain in your place of joy, you must recognize that their behavior is about something happening with them. It only has to become your problem or difficulty if you allow it to be so.

If you are concerned about the person's behavior and attitude, then you will not desire mental or emotional distance. That is fine. Just recognize you are making a decision to continue interactions with this person because of your interest and intent. The other person may not desire your help or concern and may not respond with appreciation.

When you focus on what your intentions and expectations are in each interaction, you are better able to manage your responses. If your focus is to maintain joy in your life, make a pact with yourself that you are not going to allow someone's unhealthy thinking, way of being, need for dysfunction, or actual dysfunction to upend your peace and harmony. When you are relating to someone who is having difficulty

Rosell L. Jenkins, PhD

in their life, know they may say or do some things that are a result of their difficulty. How you respond to this behavior and whether it significantly impacts your feelings about yourself or the other person will depend on how well you maintain your zone of joy. If you are cultivating healthy thoughts and have a strong positive sense of yourself, you will be able to joyfully interact with others (most of the time), despite their temperaments, bad days, or issues. *Commit to your well-being. Commit to intentional joy.*

5

CHAPTER

Early in the morning start of a new day. I wonder how life will surprise me today. It's a beautiful day. I'm going to do my part to make this a wonderful day.

Lyrics from "Beautiful Day" by India Arie

Expect Joy and Wonder Each Day

The day does not just happen to you. You make choices and that begins the moment you awaken. Stop and think right now about the questions that follow:

- How do you wake up in the morning?
- Are you excited by the promise and possibilities a new day brings or do you wake up with dread and fear?

I hope it is the former. If it is the latter, take a moment and reflect on why this is. It's often helpful to write about the process of how your day begins to see where you can make changes.

- Are you dreading your day because you are already thinking about your many tasks?
- Are you feeling overwhelmed, less than capable, irritable, or alone?

Any of these feelings or predicaments can be remedied and that is the promise a new day holds. If you did not accomplish something you wanted to do yesterday, you have the opportunity to do so today. Choose to pace yourself. Choose to enjoy your breakfast or drink your coffee/tea leisurely. Choose to do that which will fuel you most efficiently throughout the day. This will help you to operate at a steady, even, and contented pace.

First, prepare your mind for converting your possibilities into action potential and then act. There was a song I learned in either kindergarten or bible school. I didn't know it at the time, but I now know that it's a children's song by the Gaither Vocal Band. It goes like this, "I am a promise. I am a possibility. I

Rosell L. Jenkins, PhD

am a promise with a capital 'P.' I am a great big bundle of potentiality. I am learning to hear God's voice and I am trying to make the right choices...."

Visiting with my grandmother when I was younger, I would observe her rising early in the morning, generally while the house was still silent, to kneel and pray. She also kneeled and prayed at night. We knew not to disturb her during these times and to be very quiet. In fact, I only happened to know she was up so early, because I was out of the bed either to use the bathroom or to get some water. From an early age, I knew it was an important and sacred time for her. As I grew older, I also learned it was her source of sustenance.

When I awake in the morning, I greet the day and I give thanks for the day and all of its possibilities. I take a moment to pause and notice the stillness. Usually, I hear birds chirping. As I awaken early, they are usually the only other creatures stirring. I love this time of the day. Everything is before me, and I take time to notice and appreciate it. At this point in my day, I am able to shape it however I like.

If you begin each morning connecting with God/Spirit/Your Inner Voice and fully aware you are the promise filled with potential, you will make the best choice for you in that moment, that day, and you will feel invigorated and joyful. Each choice you make will be the right choice for you. It will be an intentional choice based on divine guidance. In listening to and connecting to that voice, whatever you choose will bring you joy. You may be wondering how to connect to your inner voice or decide on the next best choice.

What works for me and many others is having quiet time or time to meditate and reflect and connect with my most heartfelt desires and listening for that internal guidance that directs me to the next best step(s). You may connect with music and dancing. You may connect over a cup of coffee or your morning run. Whatever, wherever, or however it is for you, you must take time to identify it and make your connection to your promise, and ultimately your joy, intentional. Make a plan to connect and execute your plan. Your plan can be as elaborate or as simple as you desire. I recommend you keep the steps of your plan manageable—bite-size so to speak—and you take one bite at a time. Your plan may start simply with getting up earlier to have ten minutes of quiet time

Rosell L. Jenkins, PhD

to yourself. Your plan may involve stretching nightly. Choose one thing at a time that you want to change and implement that change. In a week or two, after establishing consistency, implement another change. So often we try to juggle multiple tasks because our lives are so busy and hectic, and we feel that we must get many things done. Also, we use more and more technology and are constantly tethered to it, even as we are trying to do other things. We continue to do this, despite all the research in the past years indicating that multi-tasking compromises our productivity and reduces our ability to tune out distractions. In fact, Stanford researchers have shown that multitasking reduces performance, efficiency, and IQ.

It is important to be mindful and aware of how you begin your mornings and to take time to be still and intentional. Being mindful simply means that you are aware of everything you are doing as you are doing it. You are noticing your feelings, your thoughts, and your surroundings about your present actions. You do not have to pray or believe in prayer or meditation, though I believe they are powerful tools. It is still necessary to take time to reflect and be still, to center yourself and to acknowledge all the opportunities to create joy in the unfolding of your day.

If you feel pressured from the moment your eyes pop open in the morning and are constantly operating at a hurried, harried, breakneck pace, restructuring of your day is a necessity. You may have to go to bed earlier, spend less time watching television, or choose your clothes and prepare your lunch the previous night. Everyone has moments of feeling tired, overwhelmed, and time-crunched. The way you know this is a problem is that you feel this way *more often than not.* It bears repeating that this is an indication you need to restructure the activities and priorities in your life.

I often hear people say they do not have time to exercise or to eat breakfast or to meditate, or take a vacation, or sleep, etc, etc. Essentially, they are saying they do not have time to care for themselves. Taking time for and care of yourself enables you to perform optimally, to be at your best, to intentionally create your joy. You do not let others or circumstances do that for you. You shape your life in a way that helps you maintain balance and optimal health in all areas.

Rosell L. Jenkins, PhD

You, and only you, have the power to do this. If you have to wake thirty minutes earlier, each morning, so you have time for yourself, then do it! Take stock of how you are really spending your time. Is the way you spend your time consistent with the activities that bring you joy? For example, are you really obtaining joy by watching one more reality TV show or the evening news? Or is doing this creating more anxiety for you? If it is part of your relaxation, then go for it! If you notice feelings of discomfort, uneasiness, or worry increase after watching a particular television program (e.g., a crime show), eliminate that program from your viewing schedule. Maybe more comedy and less drama is the key you need to restructure your life.

Look at how you spend your time and examine your thoughts and feelings as you engage in these activities. Do you think you are doing something worthwhile or is it just an activity to "kill time?" Do you feel satisfied and content or anxious and restless? Are you enjoying it right now, immediately? Perhaps you are enjoying the knowledge of the eventual outcome of an activity or what an activity will bring you (for example, the benefits of exercise or school or working at a particular job). Even if working at your job feels like drudgery or your schoolwork seems tedious, you can still create joy in those settings and activities.

Your intention is the key. If you remain focused on why you are having an experience or completing a task and appreciate that engaging in said task is a step towards your realizing your goal, you can stay focused on your joy. You can also focus on aspects of your job or school experience you enjoy—such as the people. If you are thinking, *I don't even like the people*, challenge yourself to find aspects about the experience that you enjoy and remain focused on those aspects. Looking for the "silver lining" will be beneficial to you. A change in attitude alters every situation. You decide if the alteration is positive or negative. **Intentionally create joy!**

Rosell L. Jenkins, PhD

6
CHAPTER

Mediocrity is self-inflicted. Genius is self-bestowed.

—Walter Russell

Smell the Flowers, Don't Linger in the Poop

One day as I was walking with my dogs, I observed that one of my dogs, Smokey, was sniffing another dog's excrement, as dogs are prone to do. Although this is what he was doing this day, I have also observed Smokey previously sniffing flowers. When I saw him lingering over the poop, I said, "Smell the flowers, Smokey, not the poop."

Occasionally, we will encounter poop. Sometimes, it will seem we have stepped in heaps of it and it is everywhere. It happens to all of us. Sometimes, we have what we consider a poopy day. In reality, what we have is a frustrating, terrifying, unexpected, or embarrassing moment. It is just that we decided to linger in the bad event. We thought about it over and over again until everything around us seemed to be negative.

Let's say you spill coffee on yourself as you are headed to work and you have to go home to change your clothes. You now realize you are going to be late for your morning meeting. Consequently, you began to feel anxious because you were hoping to arrive a few minutes early to gather your materials and prep for the meeting. If you continue to feel anxious and focus on how your morning has gone all wrong, you are likely to make another mistake and forget something else. This will further confirm to you that the day is going "badly."

You can turn things around by reminding yourself that the spilled coffee and returning home are just bad past moments. If you are able to remain in that moment of realization, then you are more likely to think through the next thing you need to do, to reorient, and to get your day back on track. For instance, you may phone a colleague and ask them to gather your materials or you may go over your comments as you are dressing and driving along in your car.

Rosell L. Jenkins, PhD

Your perception determines your day. When one thing goes wrong in your day, you have to remind yourself of all the things that have gone right. Many humans have a tendency to linger on negative events. Some research has indicted that our brain tends to store negative information more quickly than positive information. However, we are able to store positive information; we just have to work a little harder to do it. While it is more work, it is certainly more rewarding. Research has shown that you change your brain in positive ways, such as having a greater capacity to access positive feelings and to retain positive memories, when we consciously make the effort to notice the good things in our lives. If you are able to hold on to small victories, even those that occur in the course of the day, you are more likely to be encouraged and are that much closer to living joyfully. You also change your brain in positive ways by focusing on more positive thoughts and feelings.

For example, when I was younger, I had to repeatedly be reminded to do my chores. I complained about having to do chores and thought it was rather unfair that I was made to do them. I am sure this is a sentiment shared by many children, as it is a common topic in therapy. In fact, I remember a fourteen-year old male once telling me and his parents, in no uncertain terms, that he would never do chores when he was older because he would hire someone to clean for him. He was adamant about this despite being unable to identify any other future life goals for himself.

As an adult, I grew to appreciate just having time to clean my house. This was particularly true after my son was born, and the two of us were living alone. As a single working mother, I found it challenging to engage with my son and attend to his needs while trying to accomplish household tasks. Anyone with a toddler knows this struggle all too well, I am sure. I found I was so grateful to have time to maintain my home on the weekends that he spent with his father. I never would have guessed, when I was a child, that I would appreciate having time to do laundry, sweep my floor, and clean my dishes. Moreover, as much as I was grateful for the time and opportunity to tick some things off my to-do list, I was especially grateful for time to engage in activities that nurtured me, such as reading, taking a walk, meditating, or watching an

Rosell L. Jenkins, PhD

episode of my favorite show. Engaging in pleasurable activities and being intentional about it helped me maintain my joy and prevented me from feeling overwhelmed and burdened by life's daily stresses.

It is so great when we are able to do what we want to do. To even have the time or to be able to make the time to do what you really want to do is a gift. It is a gift you deserve. Remember, *you can only take care of others well if you take care of yourself.* Even with the best of intentions, you are going to fail if you do not give proper care and attention to yourself. You are going to be too tired or too overwhelmed or too busy with multiple tasks.

The best gift you can give others is to create a life for yourself that is intentionally joyful and peaceful. This makes it easier to give of yourself and your time. Then, when you give of your time or talents, it does not feel like a burden. It will come so naturally and easily that you may not even recognize you are doing it. Taking care of yourself has a positive, ripple effect and encompasses those around you. They want some of what you have and they create intentional joy in their lives and pass it on to others. In her book *Sacred*

Intelligence, Dr. Terrlyn Curry Avery discusses the need for us to focus more on our self, which she calls developing a selfish intimacy, to increase our healthy well-being and greater capacity for love.

One day as I was writing, I noticed my body was aching from exercising the previous day and I had some mild physical ailment impacting my ability and desire to write. In fact, I felt that writing caused me more pain. I made a conscious effort to relax my grip on the pen and to experience joy in the midst of my physical aching. I thought: "The day is ahead of me and it holds opportunity and promise. I am grateful I have this time and am able to write. I am grateful my hand and mind are working."

This is the way I begin my day. I intentionally notice all that is working for me, and I make a conscious effort to effectively use that which works for me. I also notice what does not work for me. Of course, everything does not work. This comes up in my life, just as it will come up in your life. We generally know when something is not working because we get indicators—just as some cars will give you indicators when something is not quite right or your car needs servicing.

Rosell L. Jenkins, PhD

Being irritated, angry, or stressed does not work very well for me. I am prone to make errors in judgment and behave in unproductive ways if I remain in these states for multiple hours in a day. When I am feeling that way, I go to the source: I examine my thoughts. It is not a person or a situation. It is what I am thinking about this person or the situation. It is what I am allowing to happen with this person or situation. At any time, I can make a different decision or have a different thought. I can think: *Exercising more is good for my body and the pain I feel when I began an exercise regimen will eventually decrease. Exercising makes me stronger and will ultimately increase my energy so I can write more, which is something I really enjoy.* Thinking that thought changes my attitude about the pain I feel from exercising and the impact I believe it is having on my writing. This encourages me to keep exercising and to focus on the pleasure I get from writing. Thinking differently produces a different feeling which leads to a different behavior and outcome.

7
CHAPTER

Don't follow the path. Go where there is no path and start a trail.

—Ruby Bridges

Believe in Your Ability to Know What Works Best For You

Make rules that work for you. Know you have had the experiences and been given the information to determine what works best for you. You receive cues that guide you as you are making a decision, and it is important to attend to these cues and recognize them as your internal wisdom.

We are flooded with information daily about what to wear, what is in and what is out, and even what to think about ideas and people. It is difficult to sort through all of this information. It is made even more difficult when we lack trust in our ability to determine what works best for us, because we are fearful of making a mistake. We are fearful of what others will think or say about us.

Many of our fears, worries, and insecurities are a function of our imagination. Sometimes, people are afraid of things that have never happened to them. At other times, they are afraid of something that happened to them many years ago and has not happened again since that time. This is especially true in relationships. Sometimes, when I am talking with a client about what they think about themselves, they will tell me things they heard others say about them during their childhood. For example, a person may believe she is unlikable and cannot maintain friendships because someone teased her in sixth grade saying, "No one will ever like you. That's why you don't have any friends." Another client may recall his college sweetheart was unfaithful and now he does not feel any woman is trustworthy. He admits he has been constantly suspicious of his romantic partners in all of his future relationships, causing distance in his relationships and, ultimately, driving away his partners.

In both of the above examples and in other similar stories I have heard over the years, I am always struck by how much influence people allow **ONE** person or experience to have on the trajectory of their life. People give up control of their life and limit their possibilities because of an experience with a bully, an immature child, or a confused young adult. As adults, our expectations of children, teens, or young adults are guided and tempered by the knowledge of their maturity and developmental level. However, when we are replaying the tapes of old wrongs in our heads, we take things said to us by individuals to be absolute truths, despite their age, maturity, or other personal issues. When you look back over your life and evaluate your fears and your negative thoughts, about you and your abilities, reflect on whether these thoughts were your conclusions based on multiple data sets or simply someone else's tape playing in your head.

One way of knowing what works best for you is being mindful of your feelings as you are going about your day or engaging in activities. Pure, unadulterated joy, not to be confused with pleasure (a momentary sensation derived from an external source), is a green light. Worry or guilt is an indication of caution. These feelings suggest ambivalence. This ambivalence may stem from old data or it may be your internal wisdom highlighting information you need to take some time to sort through. It may be an indication you are veering away from your best path. Only you can determine that by taking time to be still and in touch with whatever messages you are receiving. Consistent, debilitating pain is a red light. This is not to say that you will not experience any pain in life and that some true paths will not lead to pain. This is a time to be discerning about the pain. If you engage in an activity or are with a person and you feel pain every time, then you need to stop and assess the situation.

For example, when I began learning to play tennis, after my first game, I experienced significant physical pain. I did not want to experience this pain again, but I wanted to continue playing tennis. Thus, I had to stop and assess why I was in so much pain. I realized I was experiencing such intense pain as a result of my poor form. I was gripping the racket too tightly and positioning my arms and body incorrectly. If I had continued in the same way, my pain would have continued.

Experiencing pain could have stopped me in my tracks and I could have said, "This is not for me." However, I would have missed out on the internal joy that learning a new sport, and persisting with it until I got better, brought me. I did not let the pain frighten me. I used the pain as a guide: I evaluated what aspects of my game needed modification. The same method can be used with relationships, jobs, or other experiences. While none of us like to experience pain, we know we will experience it at times. We do not need to fear it. A healthy approach is to evaluate what is causing your pain and make necessary adjustments. If a relationship is consistently causing you pain and you have attempted sound, reasonable remedies that are not working, this may be an indication the relationship is not for you.

When my marriage ended, I was able to move beyond the pain, maintain a positive outlook on relationships and love because I knew I had worked hard and made adjustments to make my relationship work. I had looked at my behavior and modified it accordingly. My former husband and I had sought professional help through marriage counseling on more than one occasion. Thus, when the relationship ultimately ended, I was not plagued with doubts and fears. I trusted I had what I needed to make the best possible decision and to weather that decision. You also have everything you need to make the best possible decisions for your life. Knowing that is an essential part of cultivating intentional joy.

———•+•••———

Rosell L. Jenkins, PhD

8
CHAPTER

Do not be embarrassed by your failures;
learn from them and start again.
                    —**Richard Branson**

Rosell L. Jenkins, PhD

Remove Obstacles to Your Joy

Being able to return to your place of contentment and joy is key to sheltering within during any storm. It is where you feel centered and connected. It is where you feel grateful to be you. In fact if you are not feeling this way, do a mental scan. Figure out what is blocking your joy and remove that obstacle.

Most likely, you are your biggest obstacle. You have convinced yourself that you cannot or will not get whatever you desire because you think "Good things never happen to me." Or you think you just have bad luck or have been dealt a bad hand in life. The list of negative, external reasons for why your life is as it is may be endless.

Know this: you **DESERVE** for good things to happen to you! In fact, we all do. Another person's life circumstances are not an indication they are more deserving of good things than you are and there is not a limited number of good things in the world. Somehow, we get that idea. We think, "If Bob secures a great job with wonderful compensation and benefits, it cannot possibly happen for me." Whatever you want, you can have. You have to decide two things:

1. What do you really want?
2. Is the thing you think you want, the thing that will bring you joy and fulfillment?

That is why it is important to make the best choice for you in the moment. You can and will likely get what you want. Think about that for a while. I am sure there have been times you have gotten exactly what you wanted or predicted for your life. For example, you may really desire to have a romantic relationship with a particular person, but perhaps you have not invested much time in thinking why you want this person and what having

Rosell L. Jenkins, PhD

this person will mean for your life. You just know this is your strong desire. Let's go one step further and say you finally are successful in establishing a relationship with this person (or you get your dream job or purchase your dream car, etc, etc).

Did your life change? Did your mood change? How did your interactions with others change? Did you feel joy? If so, how long did it last?

Perhaps, you simply felt good you had accomplished your goal. Accomplishing your goal gave you a sense of confidence and pride. Accomplishing your goal made you feel happy. That is absolutely wonderful if that is what happened. It also may have turned out that after you accomplished that goal your life did not change in the way you had anticipated. That is because no one thing or person can bring you lasting joy. However, intentional joy arises from deliberation. So if you achieve something through discipline, determination, perseverance, it is worth celebrating. It is worth it to pause and dwell on that moment so you can recall it when you encounter an obstacle, disappointment, or failure. Recalling your achievements and victories and the internal traits that got you to that moment is how you know you have what it takes to find and maintain your joy. The joy is in the recognition you have all the internal components, whatever you need, to meet any challenge.

What matters is how you pursue your goals and how you limit or expand yourself in the pursuit of your goals. For example, if you are going to be disciplined and achieve a goal or exhibit determination to win a victory, you may have to give up idle time and expand practice time. That is okay! But let's say you begin to practice daily and you feel burnt out. You no longer feel joy when you are running or playing the piano or whatever it is you have decided to pursue. This is an indication to you that you need to shift your focus temporarily. This is the way your body and spirit speaks to you.

I am not advising you to lose sight of your goals altogether or to drastically alter your regimen. What I am advising is you may need to limit or expand an aspect of your regimen. You may need to give yourself a short break or vary the way in which you practice. You may need to add meditation time to reflect on why pursuit of this goal or activity brings you joy.

Rosell L. Jenkins, PhD

Sometimes we become so focused on achieving perfection at an activity or reaching a particular outcome that we miss the pleasure and joy in what we are doing. *Intentionally retain your joy.*

When I was applying for graduate school many years ago, I believed I had the necessary criteria to be successful in a graduate program. I had performed very well academically during my undergraduate education and had even worked on a few research projects. I thought my performance on graduate entrance exams was average but sufficient to get me into a graduate program. Moreover, I knew I was hardworking, determined, and persistent. And of course, I communicated all the reasons why I was a good candidate on the essay portion of my applications. When I received my first response from a graduate school, I opened the letter excitedly. It was a rejection letter. I was disappointed but not discouraged. I had applied to many of the best graduate programs for clinical psychology. Surely, I would get accepted by one of them, I thought. By the time I received my last rejection letter, my seventh I believe, I no longer had that thought. In fact, I was not even surprised. Having received six previous rejection letters, I knew a thin envelope held a rejection letter.

I was sad and I am sure I cried. What never crossed my mind was to give up and say graduate school was not for me. After a little time had passed, I thought about what I needed to do to reach my goal. At that time, I didn't know much about cultivating joy. What I knew was I had to refocus and regroup. I knew I was going to graduate school and I stayed focused on this, even as my plan A (attending graduate school) fell through, necessitating that I immediately come up with a plan B (work for a year prior to attending school). I was initially saddened but I did not panic. I found employment and I evaluated what I needed to do to successfully gain admittance the following year. I made contacts with people at universities at which I intended to apply during the year I was working. The next year, I was successful in gaining admission to a graduate program in clinical psychology. In retrospect, the year off was good for me and gave me perspective and insight I might not have had. Even when my program was challenging, I remained focused on my goal to earn my degree. I was able to begin the process

Rosell L. Jenkins, PhD

of knowing what really defined my joy and how to retain it by having experiences of disappointment and adversity. These experiences helped me figure out what I needed to redirect and reorient myself when I encountered discouragement or disappointment.

Sometimes when people are met with adversity, disappointment, or failure, they stop. Clients with whom I work often tell me they remain in a job they find unfulfilling or in an unhealthy or unsatisfying relationship because they are afraid of the unknown, of making a change in their life. They say, "I don't like to fail," or "I don't like rejection." No one likes it! However, people who successfully pursue their goals realize rejection and failure are just stepping stones, albeit slippery, discomfiting stones, to reaching a goal. An article in *Business Insider* discusses a postcard received by David Kerpen, an author and a CEO. The postcard was from another CEO and highlighted the differences between successful and unsuccessful people. One message on the card is that successful people embrace change as opposed to fearing it. As I mentioned earlier, part of the innate joy that comes from accomplishing a goal is know you have what it takes to get the job done. That does not usually arise from feeling the job was done easily, or necessarily, quickly. Remember, you have not always felt this way and recall when things did work out for you. They have at some point. You may have to dig deep and pay very good attention as you are sorting through your life to remember this. You may even have to wade through some muck to get to a memory of a better time, better thoughts, and better outcomes. Who you are—your dreams, your hopes, your strengths, and your ability to have joy and create it intentionally—resides inside of you.

If you are having negative feelings over a long period of time, return to some of the questions mentioned in previous chapters:

Has feeling this way for this long benefited me? Short-term, negative emotions, can serve as good indicators. They can help you redirect, refocus, or retool. Over the long-term, they can have deleterious consequences. You can get stuck in a cycle of negativity and become paralyzed with fear. You start to expect everything will be negative and not trust your judgment. ***Do not let this happen to you.*** If it already has, recognize it is a deception. Finally, if you

Rosell L. Jenkins, PhD

are unable to get yourself out of this pit of negativity, seek professional help.

"That's not fair," is a constant refrain I hear, particularly in my line of work. I hear this from children and adults. I am always a bit surprised when I hear this statement from adults. I think and sometimes say, "So what?" So what if life isn't fair or you have experienced an injustice? It happens to everyone who goes about the business of living. **Everyone**, regardless of race, creed, or even socioeconomic status, is on the receiving end of some life circumstance that strikes them as particularly unfair. Marriages end, children die, people contract fatal illnesses, wars rage, and innocent bystanders get hurt or worse. When these things happen on a large scale, they can be devastating. When we experience minor injustices, we may find it frustrating at the very least and enraging at the most. Whatever you experience, the hope is it will not permanently emotionally debilitate or paralyze you. My hope is you will realize more clearly the need for you to be intentional in cultivating and maintaining your inner joy. Intentional joy is your weapon against unfairness. If you allow the indignities, injustices, and unfairness that occur to change you fundamentally, to have you peering around corners, as opposed to fully engaging in life, then all the negative feelings, like hopelessness, will spread like an infection. This negativity colors every area of your life until all things begin to look bleak.

Unfair things happen to all of us. Some of this unfairness is worse than others. One day, as I was driving home, I heard a story on National Public Radio (NPR) in which a book detailing the stories of people suffering wrongful incarcerations was high-lighted. One of those stories was discussed in detail. The NPR segment featured the story of Jerry Miller who had spent over 25 years of his life behind bars for a crime that he did not commit. He had been released from prison by the time that DNA evidence exonerated him of this crime. I felt sad and outraged as I was listening to this story. Later, reflection on Mr. Miller's explanation of how he managed to stay hopeful and resist bitterness helped me work through emotions I felt, as a result of listening to that story. He said:

> *I had a life to live, so I had to choose how I wanted to live it, you know. What comes from*

Rosell L. Jenkins, PhD

*a man who is negative and basically is mad at
the world because he was wronged? ... I couldn't
function like that... You just have to accept
what has happened and grow from it. You know,
to just walk around angry, you know, in some
cases an angry old man—I mean, that's a waste
of the rest of your life... I made a logical decision
to do positive things and to think positive.*

When things that are unfair or unjust happen
to us, we have to determine how we move forward and
not get stuck in a place of bitterness or resentment.
Forgiveness is an essential component of being able to
maintain joy, as harboring negativity keeps you locked
in a place of discontentment and pain. Mr. Miller
decided that he wanted to fully experience his freedom.
Remaining in the past is not safer. It just ensures that
you remain a hostage to whatever or whoever harmed
you. That is not to say that forgiveness or releasing
the past it an easy task. It can be a difficult and long
process, but it is necessary to intentionally cultivate joy.

As life consists of ebbs and flows, wonderful
things happen as well that surprise us. We generally call
these things luck. If we take notice of the wonderful

surprises, we will probably see these experiences also happen frequently. Once you began to notice the positivity in your life, your attitude changes. When your attitude changes in ways that allow you to more fully embrace and engage with life, you will notice it has a boomerang effect. You have opened the door for light and light will indeed enter. Light cannot enter where everything is closed. So, even when you encounter challenges, be mindful that unpleasantness is temporary. This is not the sum of your experiences. Refuse to let negativity get a foothold and erode your inner joy. Be deliberate and intentional in maintaining your joy and optimism, even in the face of obstacles. It can and will benefit you. If you already feel you have nothing else to lose, this may mean life can only get better from here. As Marianne Williamson points out in her book, *A Return to Love*, when we focus on the light, we bring more of that into our world. Focusing on that which is positive and light effectively counters the darkness in our life.

———

Rosell L. Jenkins, PhD

9

CHAPTER

People are illogical, unreasonable, and self-centered. Love them anyway.

—Dr. Kent M. Keith

The Paradoxical Commandments

Courageously, Boldly, Freely Give and Receive Love

Surround yourself with love. Be love, give love, accept love, recognize love, and appreciate love. It is really okay! Love is always positive. Its effects are positive. Loving and responding with love does not make you weak. It is just the opposite. Loving is a sign of strength and confidence. Love improves everything and has amazing healing powers. Decide you will be the love you want to see in others and you desire to see in the world. Even when it is challenging, love intentionally. When a situation inspires anger or confusion or some other negative emotion, intentionally look for the love in the situation. While you may not be able to find it outside of yourself or with someone else, you can find it within yourself and look at the situation through a different lens. Remember, your actions are not dependent on someone else's actions or on an outcome. You love because you choose to do so and it brings you pure, unadulterated joy. You love without expectation but with appreciation for your ability to do so. This may be your biggest challenge yet, but I know you are up to it.

In my years working to help others see the best in themselves and live and love joyfully, I had many encounters that have facilitated my growth and understanding of what connects us all. I am ever reminded of the need for love and the need for us to be expressions of love. One day, early in my career, I was preparing to see a client, whom I had little confidence that I would be able to assist. My perceptions were not based on interactions with the client. Rather, they were based on ill-informed, preconceived notions, as you will learn from the story that follows.

The woman in my waiting area appeared to be in her early to mid 30s. My attention was immediately

Rosell L. Jenkins, PhD

drawn to her brightly colored hair and multiple tattoos covering her body. My assistant had provided me some background information that made me question, even before seeing or meeting this client, if she would be open or insightful regarding the therapy process. For example, she told me that the client had difficulty understanding/completing the office paperwork. I admit, at the outset, I wasn't feeling very hopeful about our ability to work together.

Maisie was very nervous when the session began. She admitted this was her very first time seeing a psychologist and that she was not even sure how to start. Wanting to ease her discomfort and reassure her, I explained that she could start anywhere she liked or that I could ask her more questions to help her begin. In response to a few prompts, Maisie detailed her difficult childhood with parents who were neglectful because of their mental health and addiction issues. No one cared what she did or how she did it, Maisie revealed. She said that she struggled academically and dropped out of school early. Maisie described relationships fraught with physical and emotional abuse. She had a low opinion of herself and her abilities. Her lack of education was a source of shame for her. She felt unable to gain others' respect or to have her opinion valued because of her background and lack of education. She desired to change her life but wasn't sure how to do so. I knew that the first step was to help her change her view of herself and I assured her that we could begin this work together.

Everything I thought, when I saw Maisie in my waiting room, went out of my head as she told me her story. She reminded me of some universal truths. We all want to be really heard. Feeling that you matter and add value gives our lives meaning. As I extended my hand to shake Maisie's hand at the end of our first session, she embraced me. She also thanked me. I thanked her for coming in and sharing with me. I recognize that it is not an easy thing to lay your secrets and your shame bare. I feel privileged that people trust me enough to do so. It is because of this that I work hard to look past the exterior and recognize how my preconceived notions or biases might impact my ability to connect with others. To do this, I listen and focus on how wanting to receive and give love unifies and transforms us all.

Rosell L. Jenkins, PhD

My awareness of the transformative power of love and our common human bonds was deepened and solidified during my training as a psychological intern. During one of my rotations, I worked with homeless military veterans living in a residential rehabilitation setting. When I began this rotation, I was a bit nervous about it. I recalled a previous intern speaking to fellow interns as she neared the end of this rotation and crying, as she became overwhelmed with emotion at having to leave this rotation site. Her emotional response seemed so unlikely based on what I knew about the rotation. In my youthful cynicism, I figured she was just a person that cried easily. I knew many, if not all, of the veterans were recovering addicts who had lived on the streets prior to entering the program. A good percentage of them had served time in jail or prison. As I was feeling a bit nervous about the rotation, I could not imagine feeling so sad that I would be moved to cry, in front of my peers no less, at the termination of this rotation.

In my first month on the six-month rotation, I mostly listened and watched the interactions of the residents and the mental health professionals. I knew that this was a fertile learning environment but remained skeptical about enjoying the experience. I recall that one resident veteran, Mario, was a brawny, bald, silent guy who had a notorious history of a long imprisonment for committing violent crimes. Mario hardly spoke when he first arrived and attempted to keep to himself, though the setting did not really allow for this. To my nervous trainee eye, he looked menacing and I generally tried to avoid him. As with most of the residents, he relaxed more over time and socialized with other residents. I relaxed as well. I got to know him and many of the other residents very well, as sober social gatherings and outings were treatment components.

As I relaxed more, I saw the residents in their wholeness and not just their actions during their illness. In formal or informal meetings, residents would discuss their past with me, particularly things they did in the throes of their addiction. Oftentimes, these men and women, in their sobriety, were wracked with guilt over past deeds. I learned that Mario was, at his core, a very gentle, shy person. He was courteous and helpful to everyone in the program. I worked with him and many of the other residents to help them know that their addiction and addiction behavior

Rosell L. Jenkins, PhD

was just one part of their story. As Eric Butterworth reminds us in his book, *In the Flow of Life*, when you are in the tunnel, you have to remember that there is light at both ends. That rehabilitation program helped those veterans to see their way to the light and it was so rewarding, transforming, and healing for residents and staff alike to embrace that light. I, too, bawled like a baby when my rotation ended. That experience was the beginning of my understanding that joy is for everyone, no matter the circumstances.

A Course in Miracles teaches that love is the only real thing and if something or someone is not showing up as love then that lack of love is fear. Love is transformative, supreme and absolute. If you are able to look at yourself and others with love, inner joy is easily maintained. When love is unrequited or ends, you know you will manage. Experiencing persistent pain, jealousy, fear, or possessiveness are glaring warning signs that fear and not love is present. ***Do not proceed. Go another way or do a u-turn.*** If you are experiencing these emotions or are on the receiving end of these things, self-examination and reflection is warranted. Do you love yourself? Loving yourself is most important because the only way to know love, give love, and receive love in a joyful, positive, and healthy way is to truly love you.

You also may need to ask if you are interacting with and experiencing life in a loving way. When a client lamented about the unfairness of life, he was thinking about his daughter, who had suffered a traumatic accident because of someone's negligence. The man and his family were consumed with the event, despite it having happened two years prior to our meeting. This couple had become so obsessed with the circumstances leading to their daughter's accident and in their pursuits and efforts to make the world a safe place for their daughter that they were not living in the present. In their fear, they were in a state of constant vigilance, on alert to spot lurking dangers and identify everything as a potential safety threat. They were not enjoying their daughter or loving their present life.

On another occasion, I worked with a client who declared his intense love for and devotion to his girlfriend. However, he spoke of her with such venom and seemed agonized by his "love." He even remarked that he resented his girlfriend because she

Rosell L. Jenkins, PhD

used his love against him. As he was speaking about his girlfriend, who sat next to him, with a mixture of passion and venom, his girlfriend wore an amused expression on her face. She seemed pleased by her boyfriend's uncertainty, confusion, and pain. Both of these individuals did not seem to be exhibiting love. They seemed engaged in an obsessive relationship they mistook for love.

In my work, I often see people confuse obsession and fear with love. They think what they feel is so intense that it must be love. If you are constantly feeling deprived, insecure, and doubtful, that is not love. Love makes you feel good. Love does not tear you down. Love is an action. If a person is only telling you they love you but you do not feel loved, that may mean they are unaware of what love is or do not have the capacity to love in a way in which you can receive it. They may be loving to the best of their ability but it is simply not what you want or desire.

In cases where people are simply unaware of what loving is, recognize your love for that person does not have to end. However, if you are expecting reciprocal behavior, that may not happen. If you desire reciprocal behavior that may mean you need to maintain love and goodwill in your heart for that person but end that relationship to find the relationship you desire and deserve. Giving and receiving love is a wondrous, joyful activity.

When I was a young girl, we often had dogs growing up. Although we lived in a rural area, in the "country," our dogs lived in the house. People often teased us because at that time, most other country dogs were working dogs and slept outside. My favorite dog was Jeff, a German shepherd mixed breed. I absolutely loved Jeff. I think my father got him one year as a gift for me and my sister. I believed Jeff loved me and my sister, as he was very protective of us. I often felt like Jeff understood my feelings and considered him a close friend. When I was in sixth or seventh grade, Jeff died. I was devastated. In fact, the whole family was devastated. I was so sad that I didn't even attend our "memorial service" for Jeff on some land behind our house. I stayed on the couch sobbing. I decided I did not want a dog again after that. I was afraid of the pain of losing a dog again. Years passed and I never had a dog again.

Rosell L. Jenkins, PhD

One morning, during my marriage, as my husband was leaving for work, he told me we had visitors. I was a bit perturbed by this as I was still in bed. He asked me to come to the door and when I got up, there were two small dogs in our back yard. We didn't know from where these dogs had come or how they got into our fenced back yard. We ultimately ended up keeping these dogs, after trying to find their owners and checking with the local shelters. Neither I, nor my husband, had wanted a dog that year; however, our daughter told us she had wished for a dog with all her heart. To this day, I do not know from where these dogs came. But I do know they reacquainted me with my love for animals and reconnected me with a happiness that I had buried. They came probably because of my daughter's pure longing (remember we get what we ask for), but they certainly filled a need for me I didn't even know existed as I had worked so long to bury it. I was at a place in my life where I was open to receiving and reconnecting with that which I truly enjoyed.

<hr>

10
CHAPTER

You must live in the present, launch yourself on every wave, find your eternity in each moment. Fools stand on their island of opportunities and look toward another land. There is no other land; there is no other life but this.

—Henry David Thoreau

A Joy Tune-Up
Help! I've Lost My Joy

E ven after all of this, there will be times when you will still lose your joy. Not just for a moment but maybe for a day or two or three. You may have an encounter or interaction that takes you from your place of contentment or you may simply lose your cool. When this happens, stop and take a deep breath. I often use the techniques I learned while reading Thich Nhat Hanh's book *Peace Is Every Step*. I breathe and say to myself the following:

> *I breathe in and I calm myself.*
> *I breathe out and I smile.*

I am generally able to use that technique when I feel myself heading away from calmness, contentment, and comfort with my being. Other times, I go barreling down the road of discontentment and do not put on the brakes to maintain my optimal state of peace and harmony.

This happened on a few occasions when I was parenting a teenager. On one such occasion, I lost my temper with my daughter. What I recall is I felt myself getting angry. I was still married at the time, and my husband attempted to divert my attention as I'm guessing he was alerted to my rising anger by the change in my tone. I was not to be diverted and subsequently lost my temper. I yelled and soon realized I was out of my place of contentment and very far away from a state of joy. Having this awareness, I stopped. However, I remained in dialogue with my daughter and I continued to have an adverse, negative reaction to this dialogue. Thus, I removed myself from the situation.

After this encounter, I took a walk. I telephoned my girlfriend and when she asked what I was doing, I responded, "Trying to calm down." She responded,

"What did he do?" I laughed and said, "It wasn't him this time." She then said, "What did she do?" I laughed again and immediately felt calmer. As has been noted by many people, laughter is a great tonic. I also laughed because my girlfriend knows me so well.

Even in that moment, many years ago, I knew the way I was feeling and the way I responded was not really about what someone else did or said. My feelings and response were because of what I thought about my daughter's actions and behavior. It is never the situation that is causing the problem. As many cognitive-behavior researchers and psychotherapists have taught, the situation is always neutral. No person or event causes us to feel a certain way. It is our thoughts about what happens that produces a feeling. Most times, I am able to remind myself of that and remain in my place of contentment. Yet, during my marriage, I sometimes reacted or responded to my husband or daughter in a way that nurtured my feelings of discontentment. When I was able to reflect on my response and my thoughts, I became aware of where I needed continued work and growth. I did not beat myself up or make critical statements about myself. That would lead to greater discontentment. I used the information to guide me and help me return to my internal joy.

All experiences are worthwhile in that they can teach us something. We can move beyond them and grow. Oftentimes, when we stray away from a goal, we feel discouraged. We may think, "I knew I could not do this." Our negativity gets the best of us. Missing the mark is not a sign of defeat. It just means you need to steady your aim and try again. Missing the mark also means you need continued practice.

Another thing that derails us is our own general negative expectations. I hear many people declare, "I'm not negative." But when you begin to talk with them, their speech indicates they are constantly peering around the corner for the next calamity. They expect that if they feel an ache it could be cancer. They expect that they might lose their job or they expect loved ones will somehow betray them. Somehow, they have gotten the message life is about preparing for disaster. As I mentioned earlier, our brains are hard-wired to remember more negative events. This is believed to be an evolutionary holdover

Rosell L. Jenkins, PhD

from when we had to watch out for mastodons coming around the corner. We are adaptable people, which is why we are still here. It is no longer to our benefit to constantly be vigilant for danger. Being in an anxious state leads to negative outcomes physically and emotionally. When you are bracing yourself for disaster or sudden-impact, how can you be content? How can you enjoy that moment? How do you feel peaceful about anything around you?

People who have difficulty living in the moment are generally not feeling very peaceful. These are the people who are chronically anxious, depressed, or irritable. When something negative or catastrophic befalls them, this event confirms what they believed all along—that life is out to get them. *They believe: I can never be happy and happiness is an illusion.* What they fail to recognize is the role they play in creating that reality in their life.

For example, if you have a healthy relationship but have a belief that romantic relationships never work or that romantic partners are always unfaithful, you may be constantly guarded or suspicious. You may always question your partner's motivations or actions. This will lead to quarreling and a breakdown in trust. It may even cause distance in the relationship and one or both of you may forget what brought you together in the first place. Eventually, your partner may act in the very way you predicted. This is called self-fulfilling prophecy. Your actions produced what you believed would occur.

What would your life be like if you expect the best? What do you really have to lose by fully believing you can accomplish your dreams and engage with life? People will say, "What if I get hurt or what if I get disappointed?" This might happen. It is certainly a possibility. If it does happen, you will not be disappointed with yourself because you will have given it your best shot. That knowledge is powerful and liberating. When you engage and give your best effort, you are not left with nagging questions about yourself. In my experience, people recover much more quickly from being disappointed by someone else than from being disappointed by their lack of effort or ability to engage with life.

Besides, the pain or hurt that one experiences from being disappointed does not skip you simply because you decided to invest less. Thinking that is

Rosell L. Jenkins, PhD

one of the ways in which we deceive ourselves. We try to put ourselves in a protective box and then we start to feel claustrophobic or lonely or bored. We began to wonder how all of these negative feelings got inside of this nice, well-built, secure, protective box. Of course, putting yourself in a box does not keep you safe. The only human box that keeps you safe is a coffin. Thus, being in a box is no way to live.

Live your life. Intentionally, expect the best out of life and do what is necessary to create your joy. In his book, *Love is Letting Go of Fear*, psychiatrist Gerald Jampolwsky writes, "Our state of mind is our responsibility. Whether we experience peace or conflict is determined by the choice we make in how we see people and situations…" If you are striving to embody or embrace love, dignity, respect, and responsibility, be assured that others are as well. Start paying attention to this. Surround yourself with these people. They will help support you when the injustices of the world seem overwhelming and you have difficulty maintaining your inner joy.

We are not perfection, but we can be persistent. Persistence makes a difference. It creates change and it moves mountains. Persistence can also herald a movement. So if we all persist in embracing ideals that promote us as a species, that move us towards peace, dignity, self-worth, and self-love, then we will move towards those ideals for each other. It is an intentional effort. This is the intentional cultivation of joy. This effort has the power to lift us out of despair and to dissipate rage.

I recall watching the movie "Fifth Element" some years ago. In the movie, there's a character who is a perfect supreme being, known as the fifth element. The fifth element turns out to be a woman, which astonishes all of the men in the movie. Interesting, that although this being is perfect and presented as capable of saving the world, she is also characterized as fragile (perhaps this is because she is female or perhaps it is because of her great emotional capacity). Towards the end of the movie, she understands war and all the destruction it entails. She no longer desires to save the world because she thinks she will just save humankind for them to engage in more destruction. Bruce Willis' character, Corbin Dallas, says, "Love is worth saving." You may be gagging at the triteness of that statement.

Yet the statement is true: love is the only thing that will save us. If we all give up, give out, or give in, then we lose our connection to each other. We let the negativity and negative people who are disconnected from their inner joy have the final say. Their words cannot be the last words. We must continue building bridges, making connections, and committing acts of love and kindness.

Some years ago, after the devastation of Hurricane Ike, I happened to catch a story on the evening news. That I saw this story was surprising as I make a point of shielding myself from the attention-grabbing misery of the evening news. This story happened to be about a group of high school students who made a documentary on Hurricane Ike. They documented people's loss, courage, and resilience. Most importantly, they demonstrated how a community came together as one to survive, to repair, and to build. Stories like that are inspiring, uplifting, and restorative. It is important to pay as much, if not more, attention to these stories. The researcher and psychologist Rick Hanson states that noticing the positive is essential to hardwiring our brains for happiness. Even though you may have to search for positive stories in the media—one of my practices—these stories exist. They remind us of who we are and why we are here. We are the same and we desire to love. We desire to connect. We desire to give and to serve. These are the true sources of sustained inner joy.

11
CHAPTER

In the depth of winter, I finally learned that within me there lay an invincible summer.
—Albert Camus

Conclusion

Ananta Swa Bhava.

Ananta is a Sanskrit mantra I recited when I engaged in a 21-day mediation series led by Deepak Chopra and Oprah Winfrey. It means, "My true self has no limits or boundaries."

As I actively cultivate joy, I work to remind myself of this daily. The writing of this book began with the ending of my marriage. As I noted, I was determined to maintain my inner joy; and some days, that was really a struggle. I believed, even as my marriage was faltering, that relationships could be joyous and loving. I wrote my intention in my gratitude journal to have a loving, caring, relationship based on mutual respect and admiration and a bedrock of trust.

As I was writing this book and looking back through my gratitude journal to remind myself of what I did to maintain my joy during that time, I saw the entry regarding my intention for my relationship. I smiled when I saw this entry because I have that now. I almost did not have it, because of limitations that I put on myself and my life. After my divorce, I focused on taking care of me and my infant son. Financially, life was very different for me. I have a private practice and business fluctuates sometimes. There would be times when I struggled to make my mortgage payments. One time I came home to darkness and realized my electricity had been disconnected for lack of payment. There were times I had to sell jewelry to pay my son's day care fees. At times like this, I would reflect on the different landscape of my life but I worked hard to not let this different landscape put me in a funk. Instead, I would think, "This is a temporary situation and I am grateful that I can find a way to meet my financial needs, even if it means selling my jewelry." Certainly, there were rough times and moments of darkness, during this particular storm. What I paid attention to the most during these times, really as a way of survival and remaining in good spirits for and because of my son, was the assistance and support I received from others.

When I first separated from my son's father, my son was so young that one of my concerns was remaining physically healthy. I worried about what would happen if I fell ill. Who would know? How would I care for my son? I realized that worrying about some future calamity was not helpful, but I still needed to put my mind at ease. I was able to do this by confiding in my nearest neighbors about what was happening in my life personally and to request they keep their eyes on my house. This required me to open up and show vulnerability in a way in which I had not been accustomed. My concerns about the welfare of me and my son superseded privacy and ego concerns. Also, what I found was when I was felled with a minor illness (as sometimes happens to humans, even mothers), I received help from people in my circle. I did not need to worry, but I did need to share and ask for what I needed.

After my divorce, I had to make other major decisions about my life. I had to determine if I would remain in my home or sell it. Do I continue my business or do I seek traditional employment with steady pay and benefits? To help me make these decisions, I meditated. I prayed and I wrote my intention. My intention was to provide a safe, loving, nurturing environment for my son and to co-parent cooperatively with his father. That was my intention and on what I put my focus. I believed the universe would take care of the rest. Somehow, things worked. I remained in my home and I remained in business. This path has not always been easy or certain, but it remains fulfilling and continues to allow me to live the intention I set for myself. Working for myself affords me the flexibility to spend time with my son in the way that is important to me. I enjoy being able to attend his school functions, remain home and care for him when he is ill, or bring him to my office when I desire. Yes, there are trade-offs. At times, that trade-off has been financial security.

Despite this, I have been happy and I have maintained my joy. I am confident I will achieve the financial security that I desire. Towards that end, my "extra" time goes towards development of my business. Although I told myself I would begin dating

Rosell L. Jenkins, PhD

when my son was around three or four, I really did not put thought or energy into that. I was fine with an occasional random date here or there as a diversion. I did not think I had additional time or energy to devote to a relationship and did not want anything in my life that distracted me from my child or my business.

When I began talking to a long-time friend and he eventually expressed a romantic interest in me, my first instinct was to squash that interest, which is what I communicated. I told him I did not have time for a relationship and no interest in one. This had been my standard party line to any man who expressed romantic interest in me, post my divorce. My old thinking and limitations told me that relationships took away from my interests and were more of a distraction and a nuisance. I was limiting myself based on past experiences and beliefs. Even my views of this man were based on my years of knowing him and not seeing him in the present, as an ever-evolving being, which we all are. In all of the years I had known him, I had placed him firmly in the friend category, so I had some difficulty seeing him as a potential romantic partner. Other friends would ask me, "Why not him?"

I recognize now that all my answers arose from the fact that I was working with the old data from the past and not living in the now. One friend said to me, "What if this is what is meant for you and you are ignoring it and turning it down and it is just the type of relationship you desire?" So I decided to give him an opportunity. I have to say, he changed my perception of him on our first date, but really, I changed. I was open to seeing him with new eyes.

Now, in this present moment, I have what I desired and more. I have a wonderful, loving partner who cares for me and my son. He is willing to go at my pace and he supports my dreams and aspirations. I joyfully celebrate this relationship in the now, because now is what matters. This relationship has not hindered my professional growth or detracted from my commitment to my child. Prior to embarking on this relationship journey, I was happy with my life and I felt like my life was pretty joyful. I realize I, unconsciously, attempted to put a container on that joy. This experience has reinforced for me that joy is limitless and you can always add more.

Rosell L. Jenkins, PhD

Life is amazing! You are amazing! All around us are amazing things, amazing people. We get to bear witness to the amazing, loving connective moments in life, not just to the atrocities. Somehow, we tend to notice the atrocities more. Just remember, if things are not going your way at this moment, they will at the next moment. Affirm that. Act on that. Continue creating your joy. Do not wallow. Do not hide. Refuse to live in fear. As Jill Scott sings, "Keep living your life like it's golden." Now, go out and intentionally cultivate your inner joy, every day in your life, in your community, and the world!

———◆•◆•◆———

About the Author

D r. Rosell Jenkins is the founder of MW Solutions, PC, which offers emotional wellness and consulting services. She is a concierge psychologist/coach, trainer, speaker and consultant, guiding individuals and organizations to optimal decision-making and peak performance when encountering emotional difficulties, obstacles, and life challenges.

Dr. Rosell Jenkins' colleagues describe her as enlightened, insightful, peaceful, fun-loving, and direct. She lives by the message that she imparts to others: life is meant to be joyful. She is passionate about broadening people's view of what their life can be and connecting them with their ability to change their lives for the better. Dr. Jenkins offers training and seminars to organizations, groups, and corporations in which she provides tools and strategies to optimize health, maximize talents and interact with others harmoniously. As a self-described joyful living architect, her trainings and seminars help individuals identify the behavioral changes necessary to intentionally cultivate joy in their lives while functioning effectively in their personal and professional environments.

Dr. Jenkins earned her Bachelor's degree from Spelman College in Atlanta, Georgia and her M.S. and Ph.D. degrees in clinical psychology from Virginia Polytechnic Institute & State University. She completed her clinical internship at the Veterans Affairs Palo Alto Health Care System in Palo Alto, California, and a postdoctoral fellowship at the University of Texas M D Anderson Cancer Center.

Dr. Jenkins is past president of the Houston Psychological Association and a member of Delta Sigma Theta, Sorority, Inc. She enjoys traveling, good food, and

Rosell L. Jenkins, PhD

outdoor activities. Dr. Jenkins' dedication to living love and maintaining joy is fierce and unwavering. She derives her greatest joy from spending time with her friends and family, particularly her young son, and her two dogs.

———•◦••◦•———

References

1. https://news.stanford.edu/2009/08/24/multitask-research-study-082409/)
2. https://www.psychologytoday.com/blog/wired-success/201406/are-we-hardwired-be-positive-or-negative
3. https://greatergood.berkeley.edu/article/item/how_to_trick_your_brain_for_happiness
4. *Sacred Intelligence: The Essence of Sacred, Selfish, and Shared Relationships.*
5. Dr. Terrlyn Curry Avery. East Bridgewater, MA: SDP Publishing, 2015.
6. http://www.businessinsider.com/major-differences-between-successful-and-unsuccessful-people-2016-3/#-1
7. http://www.npr.org/2017/03/30/522044187/an-exoneree-shares-his-story-of-wrongful-conviction-in-anatomy-of-innocence
8. *A Return to Love: Reflections on the Principles in "A Course of Miracles."* Marianne Williamson. NY: HarperOne, 1996.
9. *In the Flow of Life.* Eric Butterworth. Unity Village, MO: Unity House, 1982.

10. *A Course in Miracles, Combined Volumes, 3rd Edition.* Foundation for Inner Peace. Mill Valley, CA: Foundation for Inner Peace, 2007.
11. *Peace Is Every Step: The Path of Mindfulness in Everyday Life.* Thich Nhat Hanh. NY: Bantam, 1992.
12. *Love is Letting Go of Fear.* 3rd ed. Dr. Gerald Jampolwsky. Berkeley, CA: Celestial Arts, 2010.
13. *Hardwiring Happiness.* Richard Hanson. NY: Bantam, 2013.

Made in the USA
Columbia, SC
25 March 2018